STRANGE POEMS
STRANGER POET

A Collection of Poetic Nonsense, Furry Friends,
and Gentle Wisdom

by

Nathan Gopen

(with Geraldine and Huxley)

For Geraldine,

and for all who see the love

behind the nonsense.

Copyright © 2025 by Nathan Gopen
All rights reserved.

No part of this book may be reproduced, stored in a retrieval system, or transmitted in any form or by any means—electronic, mechanical, photocopying, recording, or otherwise—without the prior written permission of the publisher, except in the case of brief quotations used in reviews or scholarly works.

Published by Tailstring Press
Irvine, California
www.tailstringpress.com

ISBN: 978-1-930671-01-0
First Edition

Cover and layout by Tailstring Press
Some images were created or enhanced using AI-assisted tools in collaboration with the author.

AUTHOR'S NOTE

When people think of poetry, they often imagine something serious, symbolic,
and best read with a furrowed brow and a cup of overpriced tea.
But not all poems wear turtlenecks and sigh wistfully.

This collection is for the goofballs, the cat whisperers,
the grownups who still giggle, and the kids who think
grownups should giggle more often.

It began as a playful challenge—can nonsense still mean something?
Soon it became a back-and-forth word adventure, sometimes solo,
sometimes with Geraldine, and occasionally with a certain grey tabby
whose editorial process involves stepping on the keyboard.

A few poems were shaped with the help of AI tools—
not to replace imagination, but to stretch it in unexpected directions.
We like to think of them as mildly helpful ghosts with decent rhythm.

In the end, this book is a reminder that silliness has substance,
and joy is worth writing down.

OLD DOG

The old dog groaned,
since he'd thrown his own bone
on the throne

CATAMARAN

A Catamaran with a

man with a hat

on a can

and a cat

and a rat on a fan

BANANA BREAD

A well bred banana bread

named Fred

fed Hannah who said

"Fred, you're the man who can plan

a banana extravaganza!"

Did You Know?
Fred's banana bread is so well bred, he even shares the recipe!
Mix mashed bananas, flour, sugar, butter, and egg,
Bake at 350 till golden and legendarily beg-worthy.
Top with googly eyes (after cooling!) for extra charm.

HUMMINGBIRD

The hummingbird heard

not a single word

of his mother's song,

that's why he merely

had to hum along

TRISH THE FISH

Trish the fish

got her wish

to squish, with a flourish,

the nourishing dish of quiche.

THE MIGHTY DUST MITE

A dust mite

Might just

Bite dust

🪶 *Did You Know?*
Despite his ferocious name, the Mighty Dust Mite has never actually bested a feather duster in battle. He dreams of one day opening a Michelin-starred bistro called **"Might Just Dust"** — but until then, he's content nibbling lint and hoarding fluff.

THE PHOTOGRAPHER

As a photographer

I prefer

to photograph fur

THE MOLE

A mole named Julie

Ate a bowl

Of tabouli

THE APPLE

I saw an apple

upon a pill

upon a pillar

up on a hill

THE BEAR

The bear with no hair

is in fear

you will stare

at his rear,

cause he's bare.

THE GIRAFFE

A giraffe, near a bath

on Safari

went head to head

with a member of his family

SEA ANEMONES

I see

an enemy

in many

sea anemones

THE LINT ROLLER

In all candor

I pander

to dander

THE PELICAN

The injured pelican
thought he was well again.
He stood, then slipped…
and tripped…
and fell again

TOUCANS

Two toucans,

Sam and Pam,

ate two cans

of Spam with jam

on a tram

CATS AND CATTLE

It's true the cow

Says moo, not meow

Since cattle moo

The cat should too

THE ABBEY TABBY

Oh, great!
Abby, there's a
gray tabby
in the great abbey.

THE KITTEN

This kitten

takes naps

near Britain

on maps

THE FIRE-FRIAR

Does Friar Tuck

drive a firetruck?

 **From** *The Fire-Friar*

Did You Know?
Brother Ignatius "Tuck" of the Order of Smokeless Incense once moonlighted as a volunteer firefighter. He's famous for putting out a chapel blaze using only a holy water balloon and an almond biscotti. His robes are flame-retardant, his faith? Fireproof.

KANGAROOS

Two kangaroos

banged their shoes

as they sang the blues

SWORD STONE

A sword in a stone
with a gourd and a drone
on a board with a phone
and some butter, homegrown.
Then a lady appeared
from the lake with a rake—
she laid Land O'Lakes
on a marmalade cake.

THE CHICKEN

My chicken
better quicken
before he gets sick
'n stops tickin'

THE CLAM

A scam!

He's fake.

A clam can't make

a cheesecake!

Unless he's at

a clambake

THE AWARD

My Lord!

A cat on me,

with sword,

scored an

academy award!

🏆 **From** *The Award*

Did You Know?
Sir Whiskerlot, Feline Thespian Extraordinaire, holds the record for most dramatic hairballs per scene. His Oscar-winning performance in *"Clawrence of Arabia"* included a 14-minute monologue delivered entirely in meows, tail flicks, and one well-timed sneeze. He dedicates every role to tuna.

LAST RESORT

A seaside resort

is a sort

of short fort

with a port

ABOUT THE AUTHOR

Nathan Gopen has always been a little obsessed with words, whiskers, and wonder. A software developer by trade and a storyteller by nature, Nathan has spent decades dreaming up worlds both digital and poetic.

He lives in Southern California with his brilliant wife Geraldine, his clever cat Huxley, and an ever-growing archive of animal-themed wordplay. This is his first published poetry collection, though probably not his last.

Nathan believes that laughter is a kind of language—and that poetry, even the silly kind, can bring people together across generations. When he's not building websites, writing stories, or photographing fur (Huxley approves), he enjoys exploring how technology and art can work hand-in-paw.

TAILSTRING PRESS

This page intentionally left blank...

But oh dear, now it's not.

Hmm... despite good intentions, the fact is, as soon as one sets out to declare in print that the page is intentionally left blank, well, the very declaration of blankness un-does the blankitude.

It's a bit like Heisenberg's uncertainty principle.
Or Schrödinger's cat.

If you don't know what I'm talking about, well... neither do I.
Ask Claude.

www.ingramcontent.com/pod-product-compliance
Lightning Source LLC
Chambersburg PA
CBHW080444090526
44586CB00047B/2461